Haiku Human

Begin

Andrea Jones

BookLeaf
Publishing

India | USA | UK

Made with ❤ on the BookLeaf Publishing Platform
www.bookleafpub.in
www.bookleafpub.com

Dedication

For Vicki Lynn and Jeffrey Charles, my parents and first teachers. Our days together began among remnants of a once busy coal mining town turned bedroom community, the last stop before entering a national temperate rainforest. In 1980, nestled in the foothills of Mount Rainier, Carbonado was ordinary and quaint, with a population around 400. The dogs and kids ran loose through our town - a K-8 school (Washington's Historic District #19), a post-office, volunteer fire station, non-denominational church, and a saloon with a phone booth and hitching post. Life was simple, and quiet. I can't imagine a better place to begin.

"Home"

while i mix mud pies
dad builds this house from scratch
mom makes it our home

Preface

"I greet you at the beginning
For we are either beginning
Or we are dead"

-Wendell Berry

Acknowledgements

Mila, Eden, and Ben,

How did I get so lucky?

You are my reasons

to begin.

1. Reservation

a thousand dragons trained
how do i coax my own heart
now, from her cave

2. Age of Responsibility

"i can do this, mama"
she feels me hover, tense
first time slicing fruit

3. Notice

tiny crystal beads
caught spilling from the sky, twinkle
on moss-draped branches

4. Be Still

today i wandered
down to the edge of a pond
here i sit, still

5. Meditation

feel the breath
letting go of need to know
what's next?

6. Listen

before sunrise
i light my candle and hear
her silent burning

7. Toddlers

excruciating pace
dawdle, dawdle, down the path
banana slug life

8. After

after the rain
warm light pouring from the clouds
floods my soul

9. Nettle Harvest

alchemy of green
nourishment transformed from sting
medicine of spring

10. Bloom

her moment's approach
love unfolding as she goes
petals open, soft

11. Butterfly

sipping nectar
near the end, this could be her
last chance to begin

12. Permission

this is for you
a moment to enjoy
your life

13. Walking

walking along
this familiar path
two friends

14. First Words

finally my words
tentative as guests, arrive
in this empty space

15. Bath

with tip toes
breaking surface, tenative
ease down into
bliss

16. Adventurer

In this backpack
only things not tethered
to the comfort zone

17. To Begin

she's my mountain
in her shadow many things
i learn to be

18. let there be light

flip the switch
darkness vanishes
progress

19. Stay

sitting on this bench
here the warm wind whispers, stay -
let's both not rush

20. this, is not the end

i see your pain now
the work it takes to be here
it doesn't end like this

21. Still Beginning

once upon a time
my pen ran out of ink but still
(to be continued)